CONTENTS

Caesar Cipher Encryption

Caesar Cipher Decryption

Morse Code Translator

Vigenère Cipher Encryption

Vigenère Cipher Decryption

Number Pattern Printing

Star Pattern Printing

Pascal's Triangle

Quadratic Equation Solver

Matrix Operations (Addition, Multiplication)

Chessboard Pattern Printing

Histogram Generator

Scientific Calculator

Unit Conversion Calculator

Currency Converter

Simple Notepad

Text File Editor

Task Scheduler

Random Password Generator

File Encryption and Decryption

Word Count Tool

Character Count Tool

Email Validation

Simple Web Browser

Sudoku Solver

Simple Paint Program

Budget Tracker

Web Scraper

Currency Exchange Rates

Simple Chatbot

URL Encoder/Decoder

IP Address Tracker

Reverse a String

Number Palindrome Checker

Count Vowels and Consonants

Count Words in a String

Merge Two Strings

Split a String

Check Anagram Strings

Reverse Words in a Sentence

Check Pangram Sentence

Simple RSS Reader

Simple Video Player

Text to Speech Converter

Voice Recorder

Audio Player

Image Viewer

Quiz Game

Calendar Event Reminder

Simple IDE

Digital Clock with Alarms

Directory Size Checker

Check File Permissions

System Information Tool

Prime Factorization

GCD (Greatest Common Divisor) Calculator

LCM (Least Common Multiple) Calculator

Permutations and Combinations Calculator

Dice Simulation

Movie Ticket Booking System

Employee Management System

Bank Management System

Library Management System

Online Shopping System

Hotel Management System

Create and Read JSON Files

Temperature Conversion Tool

Distance Conversion Tool

Calculator with GUI

File Explorer

Text File Search Utility

Unit Conversion Tool

Volume Conversion Tool

Photo Viewer

Email Sender

Barcode Generator

Report Generator

Hello World Program (hello_world.vbs)

```vbscript
' VBScript Hello World Program
MsgBox "Hello, World!"
```

Variables and Data Types (variables_datatypes.vbs)

```vbscript
' VBScript Variables and Data Types
Dim myVar
myVar = "Hello"
MsgBox myVar & " VBScript!"
```

Arithmetic Operations (arithmetic_operations.vbs)

```vbscript
' VBScript Arithmetic Operations
Dim a, b, sum, product
a = 10
b = 5
sum = a + b
product = a * b
MsgBox "Sum: " & sum & vbCrLf & "Product: " & product
```

Conditional Statements (If-Else) (conditional_statements.vbs)

```vbscript
' VBScript Conditional Statements (If-Else)
Dim num
num = 15
If num > 10 Then
    MsgBox num & " is greater than 10."
Else
    MsgBox num & " is less than or equal to 10."
End If
```

Nested If-Else Statements (nested_if_else.vbs)

```vbscript
' VBScript Nested If-Else Statements
Dim x, y
x = 10
y = 20
If x > y Then
    MsgBox "x is greater than y."
ElseIf x < y Then
    MsgBox "x is less than y."
Else
    MsgBox "x is equal to y."
End If
```

Switch-Case Statements (switch_case.vbs)

```vbscript
' VBScript Switch-Case Statements
Dim dayOfWeek
dayOfWeek = "Monday"
Select Case dayOfWeek
    Case "Monday"
        MsgBox "Today is Monday."
    Case "Tuesday"
        MsgBox "Today is Tuesday."
    Case "Wednesday"
        MsgBox "Today is Wednesday."
    Case Else
        MsgBox "Another day of the week."
End Select
```

Loops (For Loop) (for_loop.vbs)

```vbscript
' VBScript For Loop
Dim i
```

```vbscript
For i = 1 To 5
   MsgBox "Iteration " & i
Next
```

Nested For Loops (nested_for_loops.vbs)

```vbscript
' VBScript Nested For Loops
Dim i, j
For i = 1 To 3
  For j = 1 To 2
    MsgBox "i = " & i & ", j = " & j
  Next
Next
```

While Loop (while_loop.vbs)

```vbscript
' VBScript While Loop
Dim count
count = 1
While count <= 5
   MsgBox "Count: " & count
   count = count + 1
Wend
```

Do-While Loop (do_while_loop.vbs)

```vbscript
' VBScript Do-While Loop
Dim num
num = 1
Do
   MsgBox "Number: " & num
   num = num + 1
Loop While num <= 5
```

Arrays (arrays.vbs)

```vbscript
' VBScript Arrays
Dim myArray(4)
myArray(0) = "Apple"
myArray(1) = "Orange"
myArray(2) = "Banana"
myArray(3) = "Grapes"
myArray(4) = "Mango"
For i = 0 To UBound(myArray)
    MsgBox "Element " & i & ": " & myArray(i)
Next
```

Array Operations (Sorting, Searching) (array_operations.vbs)

```vbscript
' VBScript Array Operations (Sorting, Searching)
Dim nums(5)
nums(0) = 5
nums(1) = 2
nums(2) = 8
nums(3) = 1
nums(4) = 9
nums(5) = 3
' Sorting the array
BubbleSort nums
' Displaying sorted array
MsgBox "Sorted Array: " & Join(nums, ", ")
' Searching an element in the array
Dim searchValue, found
searchValue = 8
found = False
For i = 0 To UBound(nums)
    If nums(i) = searchValue Then
```

```vbscript
        MsgBox "Element " & searchValue & " found at index " & i
      found = True
      Exit For
    End If
Next


If Not found Then
  MsgBox "Element " & searchValue & " not found in the array"
End If


Sub BubbleSort(arr)
  Dim i, j, temp
  For i = LBound(arr) To UBound(arr) - 1
    For j = LBound(arr) To UBound(arr) - i - 1
      If arr(j) > arr(j + 1) Then
        temp = arr(j)
        arr(j) = arr(j + 1)
        arr(j + 1) = temp
      End If
    Next
  Next
End Sub
```

Functions (functions.vbs)

```vbscript
' VBScript Functions
MsgBox "Addition Result: " & AddNumbers(5, 3)
Function AddNumbers(num1, num2)
  AddNumbers = num1 + num2
End Function
```

Function Overloading (function_overloading.vbs)

```vbscript
' VBScript Function Overloading (Not directly supported in VBScript)
' Instead, we can create multiple functions with different names
```

```vbscript
' Function to add two numbers
MsgBox "Addition Result: " & Add(5, 3)


' Function to concatenate two strings
MsgBox "Concatenated String: " & Concat("Hello", "World")


Function Add(num1, num2)
   Add = num1 + num2
End Function


Function Concat(str1, str2)
   Concat = str1 & " " & str2
End Function
```

Procedures (procedures.vbs)

```vbscript
' VBScript Procedures
Dim name
name = InputBox("Enter your name:")
DisplayGreeting name


Sub DisplayGreeting(userName)
   MsgBox "Hello, " & userName & "! Welcome to VBScript."
End Sub
```

Input/Output Operations (input_output.vbs)

```vbscript
' VBScript Input/Output Operations
Dim userInput
userInput = InputBox("Enter your age:")
MsgBox "Your age is: " & userInput
```

String Manipulation (string_manipulation.vbs)

```vbscript
' VBScript String Manipulation
Dim myString
myString = "Hello, World!"

' Displaying original string
MsgBox "Original String: " & myString

' Converting string to uppercase
MsgBox "Uppercase String: " & UCase(myString)

' Replacing 'Hello' with 'Hi'
MsgBox "Modified String: " & Replace(myString, "Hello", "Hi")
```

String Functions (string_functions.vbs)

```vbscript
' VBScript String Functions
Dim myString
myString = "Hello, World!"

' Length of the string
MsgBox "Length of the String: " & Len(myString)

' Extracting substring
MsgBox "Substring: " & Mid(myString, 7, 5)

' String concatenation
MsgBox "Concatenated String: " & myString & " VBScript"
```

Date and Time Functions (date_time_functions.vbs)

```vbscript
' VBScript Date and Time Functions
Dim currentDate
```

```vbscript
currentDate = Date()


' Display current date
MsgBox "Current Date: " & currentDate


' Display current time
MsgBox "Current Time: " & Time()


' Display formatted date
MsgBox "Formatted Date: " & FormatDateTime(currentDate, vbLongDate)
```

Error Handling (On Error Statement) (error_handling.vbs)

```vbscript
' VBScript Error Handling (On Error Statement)
On Error Resume Next
Dim num1, num2, result
num1 = 10
num2 = "abc"


result = num1 / num2


If Err.Number <> 0 Then
    MsgBox "Error occurred: " & Err.Description
    Err.Clear
End If
```

Math Functions (Abs, Sqr, etc.) (math_functions.vbs)

```vbscript
' VBScript Math Functions
Dim num
num = -5


' Absolute value
```

```vbscript
MsgBox "Absolute Value: " & Abs(num)


' Square root
MsgBox "Square Root: " & Sqr(25)


' Round a number
MsgBox "Rounded Value: " & Round(3.14159, 2)
```

Random Number Generation (random_number.vbs)

```vbscript
' VBScript Random Number Generation
Randomize


' Generate random integer between 1 and 10
Dim randomNumber
randomNumber = Int((10 * Rnd) + 1)


MsgBox "Random Number: " & randomNumber
```

File Handling (Reading, Writing) (file_handling.vbs)

```vbscript
' VBScript File Handling (Reading, Writing)
Dim fso, file, filePath, fileContent


filePath = "C:\Temp\sample.txt"
fileContent = "This is a sample text written to a file using VBScript."


Set fso = CreateObject("Scripting.FileSystemObject")
Set file = fso.CreateTextFile(filePath)


' Writing content to file
file.Write fileContent
file.Close
```

```vbscript
' Reading content from file
Set file = fso.OpenTextFile(filePath)
MsgBox "File Content:" & vbCrLf & file.ReadAll
file.Close
```

Command Line Arguments (command_line_arguments.vbs)

```vbscript
' VBScript Command Line Arguments
Dim args, i
Set args = WScript.Arguments
MsgBox "Number of Command Line Arguments: " & args.Count

For i = 0 To args.Count - 1
    MsgBox "Argument " & i + 1 & ": " & args(i)
Next
```

Environment Variables (environment_variables.vbs)

```vbscript
' VBScript Environment Variables
Dim sysEnv
Set sysEnv = CreateObject("WScript.Shell").Environment("System")
MsgBox "System Drive: " & sysEnv("SystemDrive")
MsgBox "System Directory: " & sysEnv("SystemRoot")
```

Creating and Using Objects (objects.vbs)

```vbscript
' VBScript Creating and Using Objects
Dim objFSO, folderPath, folder
folderPath = "C:\Temp"
Set objFSO = CreateObject("Scripting.FileSystemObject")
' Checking if folder exists
If objFSO.FolderExists(folderPath) Then
    MsgBox "Folder exists."
```

```
Else
    MsgBox "Folder does not exist. Creating folder..."
    Set folder = objFSO.CreateFolder(folderPath)
    MsgBox "Folder created successfully."
End If
```

Object Properties and Methods (object_properties_methods.vbs)

```
' VBScript Object Properties and Methods
Dim objShell
Set objShell = CreateObject("WScript.Shell")
' Getting current directory
MsgBox "Current Directory: " & objShell.CurrentDirectory
' Executing a command
objShell.Run "notepad.exe"
```

Regular Expressions (regular_expressions.vbs)

```
' VBScript Regular Expressions
Dim str, pattern, regex, matches

str = "The quick brown fox jumps over the lazy dog"
pattern = "\b[a-zA-Z]+\b"

Set regex = New RegExp
regex.Pattern = pattern
regex.IgnoreCase = True
regex.Global = True

Set matches = regex.Execute(str)

For Each match In matches
    MsgBox "Match found: " & match.Value
```

```
Next
```

Handling Excel Files (excel_handling.vbs)

```vbscript
' VBScript Handling Excel Files
Dim excelApp, workbook, worksheet

Set excelApp = CreateObject("Excel.Application")
excelApp.Visible = True

' Creating a new workbook
Set workbook = excelApp.Workbooks.Add

' Adding data to worksheet
Set worksheet = workbook.Worksheets(1)
worksheet.Cells(1, 1).Value = "Name"
worksheet.Cells(1, 2).Value = "Age"
worksheet.Cells(2, 1).Value = "John"
worksheet.Cells(2, 2).Value = 30

' Saving workbook
workbook.SaveAs "C:\Temp\sample.xlsx"

' Closing Excel
excelApp.Quit
Set excelApp = Nothing
```

Handling Text Files (text_file_handling.vbs)

```vbscript
' VBScript Handling Text Files
Dim fso, file, filePath, fileContent

filePath = "C:\Temp\sample.txt"
```

```
fileContent = "This is a sample text file created and written using VBScript."

Set fso = CreateObject("Scripting.FileSystemObject")
Set file = fso.CreateTextFile(filePath)

' Writing content to file
file.Write fileContent
file.Close

' Reading content from file
Set file = fso.OpenTextFile(filePath)
MsgBox "File Content:" & vbCrLf & file.ReadAll
file.Close
```

Form Controls (Buttons, Textboxes) (form_controls.vbs)

```
' VBScript Form Controls (Buttons, Textboxes)
Dim userInput

' Prompt for user input using input box
userInput = InputBox("Enter your name:")

' Display message box with user input
MsgBox "Hello, " & userInput & "!"
```

Events Handling (events_handling.vbs)

```
' VBScript Events Handling
Sub Button_Click
    MsgBox "Button Clicked!"
End Sub
```

Mouse and Keyboard Events (mouse_keyboard_events.vbs)

```vbscript
' VBScript Mouse and Keyboard Events
Dim objShell

Set objShell = CreateObject("WScript.Shell")

' Simulate key press (F5 key)
objShell.SendKeys "{F5}"

' Simulate mouse click (left click)
objShell.SendKeys "{Click}"
```

Message Boxes and Dialogs (message_boxes.vbs)

```vbscript
' VBScript Message Boxes and Dialogs
Dim response
response = MsgBox("Do you want to continue?", vbYesNo + vbQuestion, "Confirmation")
If response = vbYes Then
    MsgBox "You clicked Yes!"
Else
    MsgBox "You clicked No!"
End If
```

Input Validation (input_validation.vbs)

```vbscript
' VBScript Input Validation
Dim userInput

' Prompt for user input using input box
userInput = InputBox("Enter a number:")

' Validate if input is numeric
```

```vbscript
If IsNumeric(userInput) Then
    MsgBox "Valid number entered: " & userInput
Else
    MsgBox "Invalid input. Please enter a valid number."
End If
```

Simple Calculator (simple_calculator.vbs)

```vbscript
' VBScript Simple Calculator
Dim num1, num2, operator, result

num1 = InputBox("Enter first number:")
operator = InputBox("Enter operator (+, -, *, /):")
num2 = InputBox("Enter second number:")

Select Case operator
    Case "+"
        result = num1 + num2
    Case "-"
        result = num1 - num2
    Case "*"
        result = num1 * num2
    Case "/"
        If num2 <> 0 Then
            result = num1 / num2
        Else
            MsgBox "Cannot divide by zero!"
        End If
    Case Else
        MsgBox "Invalid operator!"
End Select
```

```vbscript
If Not IsEmpty(result) Then
    MsgBox "Result: " & result
End If
```

Currency Converter (currency_converter.vbs)

```vbscript
' VBScript Currency Converter
Dim amountUSD, rate, amountEUR

amountUSD = InputBox("Enter amount in USD:")
rate = InputBox("Enter USD to EUR exchange rate:")

amountEUR = amountUSD * rate

MsgBox amountUSD & " USD = " & amountEUR & " EUR"
```

Student Grade Calculator (student_grade_calculator.vbs)

```vbscript
' VBScript Student Grade Calculator
Dim score, grade
score = InputBox("Enter student's score:")

If score >= 90 Then
    grade = "A"
ElseIf score >= 80 Then
    grade = "B"
ElseIf score >= 70 Then
    grade = "C"
ElseIf score >= 60 Then
    grade = "D"
Else
    grade = "F"
End If
```

```vbscript
MsgBox "Student's Grade: " & grade
```

Palindrome Checker (palindrome_checker.vbs)

```vbscript
' VBScript Palindrome Checker
Dim str, reversedStr

str = LCase(InputBox("Enter a string:"))
reversedStr = ""

For i = Len(str) To 1 Step -1
    reversedStr = reversedStr & Mid(str, i, 1)
Next

If str = reversedStr Then
    MsgBox str & " is a palindrome!"
Else
    MsgBox str & " is not a palindrome!"
End If
```

Factorial of a Number (factorial.vbs)

```vbscript
' VBScript Factorial of a Number
Dim num, factorial

num = InputBox("Enter a number:")
factorial = 1

For i = 1 To num
    factorial = factorial * i
Next
```

```vbscript
MsgBox "Factorial of " & num & " is " & factorial
```

Fibonacci Series (fibonacci_series.vbs)

```vbscript
' VBScript Fibonacci Series
Dim num, firstNum, secondNum, nextNum, i

num = InputBox("Enter number of terms:")
firstNum = 0
secondNum = 1
nextNum = 0

MsgBox "Fibonacci Series:"

For i = 1 To num
    MsgBox firstNum
    nextNum = firstNum + secondNum
    firstNum = secondNum
    secondNum = nextNum
Next
```

Prime Number Checker (prime_number_checker.vbs)

```vbscript
' VBScript Prime Number Checker
Dim num, i, isPrime

num = InputBox("Enter a number:")
isPrime = True

If num <= 1 Then
    isPrime = False
Else
    For i = 2 To Int(Sqr(num))
```

```
      If num Mod i = 0 Then
         isPrime = False
         Exit For
      End If
   Next
End If


If isPrime Then
   MsgBox num & " is a prime number!"
Else
   MsgBox num & " is not a prime number!"
End If
```

Armstrong Number Checker (armstrong_number_checker.vbs)

```
' VBScript Armstrong Number Checker
Dim num, originalNum, remainder, result


num = InputBox("Enter a number:")
originalNum = num
result = 0


Do While originalNum <> 0
   remainder = originalNum Mod 10
   result = result + (remainder ^ 3)
   originalNum = Int(originalNum / 10)
Loop


If result = num Then
   MsgBox num & " is an Armstrong number!"
Else
   MsgBox num & " is not an Armstrong number!"
```

```
End If
```

Leap Year Checker (leap_year_checker.vbs)

```
' VBScript Leap Year Checker
Dim year

year = InputBox("Enter a year:")

If (year Mod 4 = 0 And year Mod 100 <> 0) Or (year Mod 400 = 0) Then
    MsgBox year & " is a leap year!"
Else
    MsgBox year & " is not a leap year!"
End If
```

Temperature Converter (temperature_converter.vbs)

```
' VBScript Temperature Converter (Celsius to Fahrenheit and vice versa)
Dim choice, temp, convertedTemp

choice = InputBox("Enter '1' to convert Celsius to Fahrenheit" & vbCrLf & "Enter '2' to
convert Fahrenheit to Celsius")

If choice = "1" Then
    temp = InputBox("Enter temperature in Celsius:")
    convertedTemp = (temp * 9 / 5) + 32
    MsgBox temp & " Celsius = " & convertedTemp & " Fahrenheit"
ElseIf choice = "2" Then
    temp = InputBox("Enter temperature in Fahrenheit:")
    convertedTemp = (temp - 32) * 5 / 9
    MsgBox temp & " Fahrenheit = " & convertedTemp & " Celsius"
Else
    MsgBox "Invalid choice!"
```

```
End If
```

Unit Converter (Length, Mass, etc.) (unit_converter.vbs)

```
' VBScript Unit Converter (Length - meters to feet and vice versa)
Dim choice, value, convertedValue

choice = InputBox("Enter '1' to convert meters to feet" & vbCrLf & "Enter '2' to convert feet to meters")

If choice = "1" Then
    value = InputBox("Enter length in meters:")
    convertedValue = value * 3.28084
    MsgBox value & " meters = " & convertedValue & " feet"
ElseIf choice = "2" Then
    value = InputBox("Enter length in feet:")
    convertedValue = value / 3.28084
    MsgBox value & " feet = " & convertedValue & " meters"
Else
    MsgBox "Invalid choice!"
End If
```

Bank Account Management System (bank_account_management.vbs)

```
' VBScript Bank Account Management System (Deposit, Withdraw, Check Balance)
Dim balance, choice, amount

balance = InputBox("Enter initial balance:")

Do
    choice = InputBox("Enter '1' to Deposit" & vbCrLf & "Enter '2' to Withdraw" & vbCrLf & "Enter '3' to Check Balance" & vbCrLf & "Enter '0' to Exit")
```

```vbscript
    Select Case choice
        Case "1"
            amount = InputBox("Enter amount to deposit:")
            balance = balance + amount
            MsgBox "Amount deposited successfully!"
        Case "2"
            amount = InputBox("Enter amount to withdraw:")
            If amount <= balance Then
                balance = balance - amount
                MsgBox "Amount withdrawn successfully!"
            Else
                MsgBox "Insufficient balance!"
            End If
        Case "3"
            MsgBox "Current Balance: " & balance
        Case "0"
            Exit Do
        Case Else
            MsgBox "Invalid choice!"
    End Select
Loop
```

Simple Interest Calculator (simple_interest_calculator.vbs)

```vbscript
' VBScript Simple Interest Calculator
Dim principal, rate, time, interest
principal = InputBox("Enter principal amount:")
rate = InputBox("Enter annual interest rate (%):")
time = InputBox("Enter time period (in years):")

interest = (principal * rate * time) / 100
totalAmount = principal + interest
```

```vbscript
MsgBox "Principal Amount: " & principal & vbCrLf & "Interest Amount: " & interest
& vbCrLf & "Total Amount: " & totalAmount
```

BMI (Body Mass Index) Calculator (bmi_calculator.vbs)

```vbscript
' VBScript BMI (Body Mass Index) Calculator
Dim weight, height, bmi

weight = InputBox("Enter weight in kilograms:")
height = InputBox("Enter height in meters:")

bmi = weight / (height * height)

MsgBox "BMI: " & bmi
```

Number Guessing Game (number_guessing_game.vbs)

```vbscript
' VBScript Number Guessing Game
Dim secretNumber, guess

Randomize
secretNumber = Int((100 * Rnd) + 1)

Do
    guess = InputBox("Guess the number (between 1 and 100):")

    If IsNumeric(guess) Then
        If guess < secretNumber Then
            MsgBox "Too low! Try again."
        ElseIf guess > secretNumber Then
            MsgBox "Too high! Try again."
        Else
```

```
            MsgBox "Congratulations! You guessed the correct number."
            Exit Do
        End If
    Else
        MsgBox "Invalid input. Please enter a valid number."
    End If
Loop
```

Tic-Tac-Toe Game (tic_tac_toe.vbs)

```
' VBScript Tic-Tac-Toe Game
Dim board(2, 2), currentPlayer, row, col, winner, moves

' Initialize board
For row = 0 To 2
    For col = 0 To 2
        board(row, col) = "-"
    Next
Next

currentPlayer = "X"
moves = 0

Do
    ' Display board
    For row = 0 To 2
        MsgBox Join(board(row), " ")
    Next

    ' Get player's move
    row = InputBox("Player " & currentPlayer & ", enter row (0-2):")
    col = InputBox("Player " & currentPlayer & ", enter column (0-2):")
```

```
    ' Check if move is valid
    If row >= 0 And row <= 2 And col >= 0 And col <= 2 And board(row, col) = "-" Then
        board(row, col) = currentPlayer
        moves = moves + 1

        ' Check for winner
        If CheckWinner(currentPlayer) Then
            MsgBox "Player " & currentPlayer & " wins!"
            Exit Do
        End If

        ' Switch player
        If currentPlayer = "X" Then
            currentPlayer = "O"
        Else
            currentPlayer = "X"
        End If
    Else
        MsgBox "Invalid move. Please try again."
    End If

    ' Check for draw
    If moves = 9 Then
        MsgBox "It's a draw!"
        Exit Do
    End If
Loop

Function CheckWinner(player)
    ' Check rows, columns, and diagonals for winning combinations
```

```vbscript
    For i = 0 To 2
      If board(i, 0) = player And board(i, 1) = player And board(i, 2) = player Then
        CheckWinner = True
        Exit Function
      End If
      If board(0, i) = player And board(1, i) = player And board(2, i) = player Then
        CheckWinner = True
        Exit Function
      End If
    Next

  If board(0, 0) = player And board(1, 1) = player And board(2, 2) = player Then
    CheckWinner = True
    Exit Function
  End If

  If board(0, 2) = player And board(1, 1) = player And board(2, 0) = player Then
    CheckWinner = True
    Exit Function
  End If

  CheckWinner = False
End Function
```

Calendar Application (calendar_application.vbs)

```vbscript
' VBScript Calendar Application (Display calendar for the current month)
Dim dt, firstDay, lastDay, row, col, currentDay

dt = Date
firstDay = DateSerial(Year(dt), Month(dt), 1)
lastDay = DateSerial(Year(dt), Month(dt) + 1, 0)
```

```
currentDay = firstDay

MsgBox "Calendar for " & MonthName(Month(dt)) & " " & Year(dt) & vbCrLf &
vbCrLf & " Sun Mon Tue Wed Thu Fri Sat"

For row = 1 To 6
  For col = 1 To 7
    If currentDay >= firstDay And currentDay <= lastDay Then
      If Weekday(currentDay) = col Then
        MsgBox " " & Day(currentDay),
        currentDay = DateAdd("d", 1, currentDay)
      Else
        MsgBox "   ",
      End If
    Else
      MsgBox "   ",
    End If
  Next
  MsgBox vbCrLf
Next
```

Simple Alarm Clock (simple_alarm_clock.vbs)

```
' VBScript Simple Alarm Clock
Dim alarmTime, currentTime

alarmTime = InputBox("Enter alarm time (HH:MM AM/PM):")

Do
  currentTime = Time()
  If FormatDateTime(currentTime, vbShortTime) = alarmTime Then
    MsgBox "Alarm! It's " & alarmTime
```

```vbscript
      Exit Do
   End If
   WScript.Sleep(1000) ' Wait for 1 second
Loop
```

Countdown Timer (countdown_timer.vbs)

```vbscript
' VBScript Countdown Timer
Dim totalTime, remainingTime
totalTime = InputBox("Enter countdown time in seconds:")
remainingTime = totalTime

Do While remainingTime > 0
   WScript.Sleep(1000) ' Wait for 1 second
   remainingTime = remainingTime - 1
Loop

MsgBox "Countdown complete!"
```

To-Do List Application (todo_list.vbs)

```vbscript
' VBScript To-Do List Application
Dim todoList, newItem

Set todoList = CreateObject("Scripting.Dictionary")

Do
   newItem = InputBox("Enter a new item for the to-do list (or type 'exit' to finish):")
   If newItem <> "" And LCase(newItem) <> "exit" Then
      todoList.Add todoList.Count + 1, newItem
   End If
Loop Until LCase(newItem) = "exit"
```

```vbscript
MsgBox "To-Do List:" & vbCrLf & Join(todoList.Items(), vbCrLf)
```

Digital Clock (digital_clock.vbs)

```vbscript
' VBScript Digital Clock
Do
    WScript.Sleep(1000) ' Wait for 1 second
    MsgBox Time(), vbInformation, "Digital Clock"
Loop While True
```

Dice Rolling Simulation (dice_rolling_simulation.vbs)

```vbscript
' VBScript Dice Rolling Simulation
Dim rollResult

Randomize
rollResult = Int((6 * Rnd) + 1) ' Roll a 6-sided dice

MsgBox "You rolled: " & rollResult
```

Simple Text Editor (simple_text_editor.vbs)

```vbscript
' VBScript Simple Text Editor
Dim filePath, fileContent

filePath = InputBox("Enter file path:")

If filePath <> "" Then
    Set fso = CreateObject("Scripting.FileSystemObject")
    If fso.FileExists(filePath) Then
        Set file = fso.OpenTextFile(filePath)
        fileContent = file.ReadAll
        file.Close
    Else
```

```vbscript
        fileContent = ""
    End If

    newContent = InputBox("Enter text:" & vbCrLf & vbCrLf & "Current Content:" & vbCrLf & fileContent)

    Set file = fso.CreateTextFile(filePath)
    file.Write newContent
    file.Close

    MsgBox "Text saved successfully!"
End If
```

Hangman Game (hangman_game.vbs)

```vbscript
' VBScript Hangman Game
Dim secretWord, guessedWord, guessedLetters, maxAttempts, attemptsLeft, letter

secretWord = InputBox("Enter secret word:")
maxAttempts = 6
attemptsLeft = maxAttempts
guessedWord = String(Len(secretWord), "-")
guessedLetters = ""

Do While attemptsLeft > 0 And InStr(guessedWord, "-") > 0
    MsgBox "Secret Word: " & guessedWord & vbCrLf & "Attempts Left: " & attemptsLeft

    letter = LCase(InputBox("Guess a letter:"))
    If Len(letter) = 1 And Asc(letter) >= Asc("a") And Asc(letter) <= Asc("z") Then
        If InStr(guessedLetters, letter) = 0 Then
            guessedLetters = guessedLetters & letter
```

```vbscript
        If InStr(secretWord, letter) > 0 Then
            For i = 1 To Len(secretWord)
                If Mid(secretWord, i, 1) = letter Then
                    guessedWord = Left(guessedWord, i - 1) & letter & Mid(guessedWord, i
+ 1)
                End If
            Next
        Else
            attemptsLeft = attemptsLeft - 1
        End If
    Else
        MsgBox "You already guessed this letter. Try a different one."
    End If
    Else
        MsgBox "Invalid input. Please enter a single letter (a-z)."
    End If
Loop


If InStr(guessedWord, "-") = 0 Then
    MsgBox "Congratulations! You guessed the word '" & secretWord & "' correctly."
Else
    MsgBox "You ran out of attempts. The word was '" & secretWord & "'. Better luck
next time!"
End If
```

Rock-Paper-Scissors Game (rock_paper_scissors.vbs)

```vbscript
' VBScript Rock-Paper-Scissors Game
Dim choices, userChoice, computerChoice, result


choices = Array("Rock", "Paper", "Scissors")
computerChoice = choices(Int((3 * Rnd)))
```

```vbscript
userChoice = InputBox("Choose Rock, Paper, or Scissors:")


If userChoice <> "" And InStr(1, "RockPaperScissors", LCase(userChoice), _
vbTextCompare) > 0 Then
    MsgBox "Computer chose: " & computerChoice
    If LCase(userChoice) = "rock" And computerChoice = "Scissors" Or _
        LCase(userChoice) = "paper" And computerChoice = "Rock" Or _
        LCase(userChoice) = "scissors" And computerChoice = "Paper" Then
        result = "You win!"
    ElseIf LCase(userChoice) = LCase(computerChoice) Then
        result = "It's a tie!"
    Else
        result = "Computer wins!"
    End If
    MsgBox result
Else
    MsgBox "Invalid choice. Please choose Rock, Paper, or Scissors."
End If
```

Phonebook Management System (phonebook_management.vbs)

```vbscript
' VBScript Phonebook Management System
Dim phonebook, name, phoneNumber
Set phonebook = CreateObject("Scripting.Dictionary")
Do
    name = InputBox("Enter contact name (or type 'exit' to finish):")
    If name <> "" And LCase(name) <> "exit" Then
        phoneNumber = InputBox("Enter phone number for " & name & ":")
        phonebook.Add name, phoneNumber
    End If
Loop Until LCase(name) = "exit"
```

```vbscript
If phonebook.Count > 0 Then
    MsgBox "Phonebook:" & vbCrLf & Join(phonebook.Items(), vbCrLf)
End If
```

Quiz Application (quiz_application.vbs)

```vbscript
' VBScript Quiz Application
Dim questions, answers, userAnswers, score, i
questions = Array("What is the capital of France?", "Who painted the Mona Lisa?",
"What is the largest planet in our solar system?")
answers = Array("Paris", "Leonardo da Vinci", "Jupiter")
userAnswers = Array("", "", "")
score = 0

For i = 0 To UBound(questions)
    userAnswers(i) = InputBox(questions(i))
    If LCase(userAnswers(i)) = LCase(answers(i)) Then
        score = score + 1
    End If
Next

MsgBox "Quiz Complete!" & vbCrLf & "Your Score: " & score & " out of " &
UBound(questions) + 1
```

Binary to Decimal Converter (binary_to_decimal_converter.vbs)

```vbscript
' VBScript Binary to Decimal Converter
Dim binaryNum, decimalNum

binaryNum = InputBox("Enter a binary number:")
decimalNum = 0

For i = Len(binaryNum) To 1 Step -1
```

```vbscript
    If Mid(binaryNum, Len(binaryNum) - i + 1, 1) = "1" Then
        decimalNum = decimalNum + (2 ^ (i - 1))
    End If
Next


MsgBox "Decimal Equivalent: " & decimalNum
```

Decimal to Binary Converter (decimal_to_binary_converter.vbs)

```vbscript
' VBScript Decimal to Binary Converter
Dim decimalNum, binaryNum
decimalNum = InputBox("Enter a decimal number:")
binaryNum = ""


Do
    binaryNum = (decimalNum Mod 2) & binaryNum
    decimalNum = Int(decimalNum / 2)
Loop While decimalNum > 0


MsgBox "Binary Equivalent: " & binaryNum
```

Caesar Cipher Encryption (caesar_cipher_encryption.vbs)

```vbscript
' VBScript Caesar Cipher Encryption
Dim plaintext, shift, ciphertext

plaintext = InputBox("Enter plaintext:")
shift = CInt(InputBox("Enter shift value (0-25):"))

If shift >= 0 And shift <= 25 Then
    ciphertext = ""

    For i = 1 To Len(plaintext)
```

```
        char = Mid(plaintext, i, 1)
        If char >= "A" And char <= "Z" Then
            newChar = Chr(((Asc(char) - Asc("A") + shift) Mod 26) + Asc("A"))
        ElseIf char >= "a" And char <= "z" Then
            newChar = Chr(((Asc(char) - Asc("a") + shift) Mod 26) + Asc("a"))
        Else
            newChar = char ' Preserve non-alphabet characters
        End If
        ciphertext = ciphertext & newChar
    Next

    MsgBox "Encrypted Text: " & ciphertext
Else
    MsgBox "Invalid shift value. Please enter a value between 0 and 25."
End If
```

Caesar Cipher Decryption (caesar_cipher_decryption.vbs)

```
' VBScript Caesar Cipher Decryption
Dim ciphertext, shift, plaintext

ciphertext = InputBox("Enter ciphertext:")
shift = CInt(InputBox("Enter shift value (0-25):"))

If shift >= 0 And shift <= 25 Then
    plaintext = ""

    For i = 1 To Len(ciphertext)
        char = Mid(ciphertext, i, 1)
        If char >= "A" And char <= "Z" Then
            newChar = Chr(((Asc(char) - Asc("A") - shift + 26) Mod 26) + Asc("A"))
        ElseIf char >= "a" And char <= "z" Then
```

```vbscript
            newChar = Chr(((Asc(char) - Asc("a") - shift + 26) Mod 26) + Asc("a"))
        Else
            newChar = char ' Preserve non-alphabet characters
        End If
        plaintext = plaintext & newChar
    Next


    MsgBox "Decrypted Text: " & plaintext
Else
    MsgBox "Invalid shift value. Please enter a value between 0 and 25."
End If
```

Morse Code Translator (morse_code_translator.vbs)

```vbscript
' VBScript Morse Code Translator
Dim morseCodeDict, inputText, outputText, char
morseCodeDict = CreateObject("Scripting.Dictionary")
morseCodeDict.Add("A", ".-")
morseCodeDict.Add("B", "-...")
morseCodeDict.Add("C", "-.-.")
morseCodeDict.Add("D", "-..")
morseCodeDict.Add("E", ".")
morseCodeDict.Add("F", "..-.")
morseCodeDict.Add("G", "--.")
morseCodeDict.Add("H", "....")
morseCodeDict.Add("I", "..")
morseCodeDict.Add("J", ".---")
morseCodeDict.Add("K", "-.-")
morseCodeDict.Add("L", ".-..")
morseCodeDict.Add("M", "--")
morseCodeDict.Add("N", "-.")
morseCodeDict.Add("O", "---")
```

```vbscript
morseCodeDict.Add("P", ".--.")
morseCodeDict.Add("Q", "--.-")
morseCodeDict.Add("R", ".-.")
morseCodeDict.Add("S", "...")
morseCodeDict.Add("T", "-")
morseCodeDict.Add("U", "..-")
morseCodeDict.Add("V", "...-")
morseCodeDict.Add("W", ".--")
morseCodeDict.Add("X", "-..-")
morseCodeDict.Add("Y", "-.--")
morseCodeDict.Add("Z", "--..")
inputText = UCase(InputBox("Enter text to convert to Morse code:"))
outputText = ""
For i = 1 To Len(inputText)
    char = Mid(inputText, i, 1)
    If morseCodeDict.Exists(char) Then
        outputText = outputText & morseCodeDict(char) & " "
    ElseIf char = " " Then
        outputText = outputText & " / "
    Else
        outputText = outputText & char & " " ' Preserve non-alphabet characters
    End If
Next
MsgBox "Morse Code: " & outputText
```

Vigenère Cipher Encryption (vigenere_cipher_encryption.vbs)

```vbscript
' VBScript Vigenère Cipher Encryption
Dim plaintext, keyword, ciphertext, keyIndex, shift
plaintext = InputBox("Enter plaintext:")
keyword = UCase(InputBox("Enter keyword:"))
ciphertext = ""
```

```vbscript
keyIndex = 1
For i = 1 To Len(plaintext)
    char = Mid(plaintext, i, 1)
    If char >= "A" And char <= "Z" Then
        shift = Asc(Mid(keyword, keyIndex, 1)) - Asc("A")
        newChar = Chr(((Asc(char) - Asc("A") + shift) Mod 26) + Asc("A"))
        ciphertext = ciphertext & newChar
        keyIndex = keyIndex Mod Len(keyword) + 1
    Else
        ciphertext = ciphertext & char ' Preserve non-alphabet characters
    End If
Next
MsgBox "Encrypted Text: " & ciphertext
```

Vigenère Cipher Decryption (vigenere_cipher_decryption.vbs)

```vbscript
' VBScript Vigenère Cipher Decryption
Dim ciphertext, keyword, plaintext, keyIndex, shift
ciphertext = InputBox("Enter ciphertext:")
keyword = UCase(InputBox("Enter keyword:"))
plaintext = ""
keyIndex = 1
For i = 1 To Len(ciphertext)
    char = Mid(ciphertext, i, 1)
    If char >= "A" And char <= "Z" Then
        shift = Asc(Mid(keyword, keyIndex, 1)) - Asc("A")
        newChar = Chr(((Asc(char) - Asc("A") - shift + 26) Mod 26) + Asc("A"))
        plaintext = plaintext & newChar
        keyIndex = keyIndex Mod Len(keyword) + 1
    Else
        plaintext = plaintext & char ' Preserve non-alphabet characters
    End If
```

```
Next

MsgBox "Decrypted Text: " & plaintext
```

Number Pattern Printing (number_pattern_printing.vbs)

```
' VBScript Number Pattern Printing

Dim rows, num

rows = CInt(InputBox("Enter number of rows:"))

For i = 1 To rows
    num = 1
    For j = 1 To i
        WScript.StdOut.Write num & " "
        num = num + 1
    Next
    WScript.StdOut.Write vbCrLf
Next
```

Star Pattern Printing (star_pattern_printing.vbs)

```
' VBScript Star Pattern Printing

Dim rows
rows = CInt(InputBox("Enter number of rows:"))

For i = 1 To rows
    For j = 1 To i
        WScript.StdOut.Write "*"
    Next
    WScript.StdOut.Write vbCrLf
Next
```

Pascal's Triangle (pascals_triangle.vbs)

```vbscript
' VBScript Pascal's Triangle
Dim numRows, row, col, currentNum
numRows = CInt(InputBox("Enter number of rows for Pascal's Triangle:"))


For row = 0 To numRows - 1
    For col = 0 To row
        currentNum = BinomialCoefficient(row, col)
        WScript.StdOut.Write currentNum & " "
    Next
    WScript.StdOut.Write vbCrLf
Next


Function BinomialCoefficient(n, k)
    Dim numerator, denominator
    numerator = Factorial(n)
    denominator = Factorial(k) * Factorial(n - k)
    BinomialCoefficient = numerator / denominator
End Function


Function Factorial(num)
    If num <= 1 Then
        Factorial = 1
    Else
        Factorial = num * Factorial(num - 1)
    End If
End Function
```

Quadratic Equation Solver (quadratic_equation_solver.vbs)

```vbscript
' VBScript Quadratic Equation Solver
Dim a, b, c, discriminant, root1, root2
```

```
a = CDbl(InputBox("Enter coefficient a:"))
b = CDbl(InputBox("Enter coefficient b:"))
c = CDbl(InputBox("Enter coefficient c:"))

discriminant = (b ^ 2) - (4 * a * c)

If discriminant > 0 Then
    root1 = (-b + Sqr(discriminant)) / (2 * a)
    root2 = (-b - Sqr(discriminant)) / (2 * a)
    MsgBox "Roots are: " & root1 & " and " & root2
ElseIf discriminant = 0 Then
    root1 = -b / (2 * a)
    MsgBox "Root is: " & root1
Else
    MsgBox "No real roots exist (complex roots)"
End If
```

Matrix Operations (matrix_operations.vbs)

```
' VBScript Matrix Operations (Addition, Multiplication)
Dim matrixA, matrixB, numRowsA, numColsA, numRowsB, numColsB
Dim resultMatrixAddition, resultMatrixMultiplication, row, col, sum

' Input matrix A
numRowsA = CInt(InputBox("Enter number of rows for Matrix A:"))
numColsA = CInt(InputBox("Enter number of columns for Matrix A:"))
ReDim matrixA(numRowsA - 1, numColsA - 1)

For row = 0 To numRowsA - 1
    For col = 0 To numColsA - 1
```

```vbscript
      matrixA(row, col) = CDbl(InputBox("Enter value for Matrix A[" & row & "][" &
col & "]:"))
   Next
Next


' Input matrix B
numRowsB = CInt(InputBox("Enter number of rows for Matrix B:"))
numColsB = CInt(InputBox("Enter number of columns for Matrix B:"))
ReDim matrixB(numRowsB - 1, numColsB - 1)


For row = 0 To numRowsB - 1
   For col = 0 To numColsB - 1
      matrixB(row, col) = CDbl(InputBox("Enter value for Matrix B[" & row & "][" &
col & "]:"))
   Next
Next


' Matrix Addition
If numRowsA = numRowsB And numColsA = numColsB Then
   ReDim resultMatrixAddition(numRowsA - 1, numColsA - 1)
   For row = 0 To numRowsA - 1
     For col = 0 To numColsA - 1
        resultMatrixAddition(row, col) = matrixA(row, col) + matrixB(row, col)
     Next
   Next
   MsgBox "Matrix Addition Result:" & vbCrLf &
MatrixToString(resultMatrixAddition)
Else
   MsgBox "Matrix Addition is not possible (matrices must have same dimensions)"
End If
```

```vbscript
' Matrix Multiplication
If numColsA = numRowsB Then
    ReDim resultMatrixMultiplication(numRowsA - 1, numColsB - 1)
    For row = 0 To numRowsA - 1
        For col = 0 To numColsB - 1
            sum = 0
            For k = 0 To numColsA - 1
                sum = sum + (matrixA(row, k) * matrixB(k, col))
            Next
            resultMatrixMultiplication(row, col) = sum
        Next
    Next
    MsgBox "Matrix Multiplication Result:" & vbCrLf & _
MatrixToString(resultMatrixMultiplication)
Else
    MsgBox "Matrix Multiplication is not possible (number of columns in Matrix A must
be equal to number of rows in Matrix B)"
End If


Function MatrixToString(matrix)
    Dim strMatrix, row, col
    strMatrix = ""
    For row = 0 To UBound(matrix, 1)
        For col = 0 To UBound(matrix, 2)
            strMatrix = strMatrix & matrix(row, col) & " "
        Next
        strMatrix = strMatrix & vbCrLf
    Next
    MatrixToString = strMatrix
End Function
```

Chessboard Pattern Printing (chessboard_pattern_printing.vbs)

```vbscript
' VBScript Chessboard Pattern Printing
Dim rows, cols, isBlack

rows = CInt(InputBox("Enter number of rows:"))
cols = CInt(InputBox("Enter number of columns:"))

For row = 1 To rows
    For col = 1 To cols
        If (row + col) Mod 2 = 0 Then
            WScript.StdOut.Write "▓" ' Black cell
        Else
            WScript.StdOut.Write "░" ' White cell
        End If
    Next
    WScript.StdOut.Write vbCrLf
Next
```

Histogram Generator (histogram_generator.vbs)

```vbscript
' VBScript Histogram Generator
Dim values, value, histogram
values = InputBox("Enter a list of values separated by commas:")
values = Split(values, ",")

Set histogram = CreateObject("Scripting.Dictionary")

For Each value In values
    If IsNumeric(value) Then
        If histogram.Exists(value) Then
```

```vbscript
            histogram(value) = histogram(value) + 1
        Else
            histogram.Add value, 1
        End If
    End If
Next


For Each key In histogram.Keys
    WScript.StdOut.Write key & ": "
    For i = 1 To histogram(key)
        WScript.StdOut.Write "■"
    Next
    WScript.StdOut.Write vbCrLf
Next
```

Scientific Calculator (scientific_calculator.vbs)

```vbscript
' VBScript Scientific Calculator
Dim expression, result
expression = InputBox("Enter a mathematical expression:")
result = Evaluate(expression)


MsgBox "Result: " & result


Function Evaluate(expr)
    On Error Resume Next
    Evaluate = Eval(expr)
    If Err.Number <> 0 Then
        Evaluate = "Error"
    End If
    On Error GoTo 0
End Function
```

Unit Conversion Calculator (unit_conversion_calculator.vbs)

```vbscript
' VBScript Unit Conversion Calculator
Dim choice, value, convertedValue

choice = InputBox("Choose conversion:" & vbCrLf & _
        "1. Feet to Meters" & vbCrLf & _
        "2. Pounds to Kilograms")

value = CDbl(InputBox("Enter value to convert:"))

Select Case choice
   Case "1"
      convertedValue = value * 0.3048 ' Conversion factor for feet to meters
      MsgBox value & " feet = " & convertedValue & " meters"
   Case "2"
      convertedValue = value * 0.45359237 ' Conversion factor for pounds to kilograms
      MsgBox value & " pounds = " & convertedValue & " kilograms"
   Case Else
      MsgBox "Invalid choice"
End Select
```

Currency Converter (currency_converter.vbs)

```vbscript
' VBScript Currency Converter
Dim amountUSD, rate, amountConverted

amountUSD = CDbl(InputBox("Enter amount in USD:"))
rate = CDbl(InputBox("Enter exchange rate (USD to desired currency):"))

amountConverted = amountUSD * rate
MsgBox amountUSD & " USD = " & amountConverted & " units of desired currency"
```

Simple Notepad (simple_notepad.vbs)

```vbscript
' VBScript Simple Notepad
Dim filePath, fileContent

filePath = InputBox("Enter file path:")

If filePath <> "" Then
    Set fso = CreateObject("Scripting.FileSystemObject")
    If fso.FileExists(filePath) Then
        Set file = fso.OpenTextFile(filePath)
        fileContent = file.ReadAll
        file.Close
    Else
        fileContent = ""
    End If

    newContent = InputBox("Enter text:" & vbCrLf & vbCrLf & "Current Content:" & vbCrLf & fileContent)

    Set file = fso.CreateTextFile(filePath)
    file.Write newContent
    file.Close

    MsgBox "Text saved successfully!"
End If
```

Text File Editor (text_file_editor.vbs)

```vbscript
' VBScript Text File Editor
Dim filePath, fileContent

filePath = InputBox("Enter file path:")
```

```vbscript
If filePath <> "" Then
  Set fso = CreateObject("Scripting.FileSystemObject")
  If fso.FileExists(filePath) Then
    Set file = fso.OpenTextFile(filePath)
    fileContent = file.ReadAll
    file.Close
  Else
    fileContent = ""
  End If

  newContent = InputBox("Enter text:" & vbCrLf & vbCrLf & "Current Content:" & vbCrLf & fileContent)

  Set file = fso.CreateTextFile(filePath)
  file.Write newContent
  file.Close

  MsgBox "Text saved successfully!"
End If
```

Task Scheduler (task_scheduler.vbs)

```vbscript
' VBScript Task Scheduler
Dim taskName, taskTime, currentTime
taskName = InputBox("Enter task name:")
taskTime = CDate(InputBox("Enter task time (HH:MM AM/PM):"))
Do
  currentTime = Time()
  If FormatDateTime(currentTime, vbShortTime) = FormatDateTime(taskTime, vbShortTime) Then
    MsgBox "Executing task: " & taskName
```

```vbscript
    Exit Do
  End If
  WScript.Sleep(1000) ' Wait for 1 second
Loop
```

Random Password Generator (random_password_generator.vbs)

```vbscript
' VBScript Random Password Generator
Dim passwordLength, password, chars
chars = "ABCDEFGHIJKLMNOPQRSTUVWXYZabcdefghijklmnopqrstuvwxyz0123456789!@#$%^&*()_+-=[]{}|;:,.<>?~"

passwordLength = CInt(InputBox("Enter password length:"))
password = ""

For i = 1 To passwordLength
  Randomize
  password = password & Mid(chars, Int((Len(chars) * Rnd) + 1), 1)
Next

MsgBox "Random Password: " & password
```

File Encryption and Decryption (file_encryption_decryption.vbs)

```vbscript
' VBScript File Encryption and Decryption
Dim filePath, fileContent, encryptedContent, decryptedContent

' Function to encrypt content
Function Encrypt(content)
  Dim key, i, charCode
  key = 3 ' Encryption key (shift value)
  encryptedContent = ""
```

```vbscript
  For i = 1 To Len(content)
    charCode = Asc(Mid(content, i, 1))
    If charCode >= 32 And charCode <= 126 Then ' Encrypt only printable characters
      encryptedContent = encryptedContent & Chr(((charCode - 32 + key) Mod 95) + 32)
    Else
      encryptedContent = encryptedContent & Mid(content, i, 1) ' Preserve non-printable characters
    End If
  Next
  Encrypt = encryptedContent
End Function


' Function to decrypt content
Function Decrypt(content)
  Dim key, i, charCode
  key = 3 ' Decryption key (shift value)
  decryptedContent = ""
  For i = 1 To Len(content)
    charCode = Asc(Mid(content, i, 1))
    If charCode >= 32 And charCode <= 126 Then ' Decrypt only printable characters
      decryptedContent = decryptedContent & Chr(((charCode - 32 - key + 95) Mod 95) + 32)
    Else
      decryptedContent = decryptedContent & Mid(content, i, 1) ' Preserve non-printable characters
    End If
  Next
  Decrypt = decryptedContent
End Function
```

```vbscript
filePath = InputBox("Enter file path:")

If filePath <> "" Then
    Set fso = CreateObject("Scripting.FileSystemObject")
    If fso.FileExists(filePath) Then
        Set file = fso.OpenTextFile(filePath)
        fileContent = file.ReadAll
        file.Close

        ' Encrypt the file content
        encryptedContent = Encrypt(fileContent)

        ' Write encrypted content back to the file
        Set outFile = fso.CreateTextFile(filePath, True)
        outFile.Write encryptedContent
        outFile.Close

        MsgBox "File encrypted successfully!"
    Else
        MsgBox "File not found"
    End If
End If
' To decrypt a file, use the Decrypt function similarly to how Encrypt is used above.
```

Word Count Tool (word_count_tool.vbs)

```vbscript
' VBScript Word Count Tool
Dim text, words

text = InputBox("Enter text:")
words = Split(text, " ")
```

```
MsgBox "Word Count: " & UBound(words) + 1
```

Character Count Tool (character_count_tool.vbs)

```
' VBScript Character Count Tool
Dim text
text = InputBox("Enter text:")
MsgBox "Character Count: " & Len(text)
```

Email Validation (email_validation.vbs)

```
' VBScript Email Validation
Dim email

email = InputBox("Enter email address:")

If IsValidEmail(email) Then
    MsgBox email & " is a valid email address."
Else
    MsgBox email & " is not a valid email address."
End If

Function IsValidEmail(email)
    Dim regex
    Set regex = New RegExp
    regex.Pattern = "^[\w-\.]+@([\w-]+\.)+[\w-]{2,4}$"
    IsValidEmail – regex.Test(email)
End Function
```

Simple Web Browser (simple_web_browser.vbs)

```
' VBScript Simple Web Browser
Dim url
```

```vbscript
url = InputBox("Enter URL:")
If url <> "" Then
   Set ie = CreateObject("InternetExplorer.Application")
   ie.Visible = True
   ie.Navigate url
Else
   MsgBox "Invalid URL"
End If
```

Sudoku Solver (sudoku_solver.vbs)

```vbscript
' VBScript Sudoku Solver
Dim sudoku(8, 8)
' Function to print Sudoku grid
Sub PrintSudoku()
   Dim row, col
   For row = 0 To 8
      For col = 0 To 8
         WScript.StdOut.Write sudoku(row, col) & " "
      Next
      WScript.StdOut.Write vbCrLf
   Next
End Sub


' Function to solve Sudoku using backtracking
Function SolveSudoku()
   Dim row, col
   For row = 0 To 8
      For col = 0 To 8
         If sudoku(row, col) = 0 Then ' Empty cell found
            For num = 1 To 9
               If IsSafe(row, col, num) Then
```

```vbscript
            sudoku(row, col) = num
            If SolveSudoku() Then
                SolveSudoku = True
                Exit Function
            End If
            sudoku(row, col) = 0 ' Backtrack
          End If
        Next
        SolveSudoku = False
        Exit Function
      End If
    Next
  Next
  SolveSudoku = True ' Sudoku solved
End Function


' Function to check if a number is safe to place in a cell
Function IsSafe(row, col, num)
  ' Check row and column
  For i = 0 To 8
    If sudoku(row, i) = num Or sudoku(i, col) = num Then
      IsSafe = False
      Exit Function
    End If
  Next

  ' Check 3x3 grid
  Dim startRow, startCol
  startRow = (row \ 3) * 3
  startCol = (col \ 3) * 3
  For i = 0 To 2
```

```vbscript
        For j = 0 To 2
            If sudoku(startRow + i, startCol + j) = num Then
                IsSafe = False
                Exit Function
            End If
        Next
    Next


    IsSafe = True
End Function


' Main code
' Sample Sudoku puzzle (0 represents empty cells)
sudoku = Array(Array(5, 3, 0, 0, 7, 0, 0, 0, 0), _
            Array(6, 0, 0, 1, 9, 5, 0, 0, 0), _
            Array(0, 9, 8, 0, 0, 0, 0, 6, 0), _
            Array(8, 0, 0, 0, 6, 0, 0, 0, 3), _
            Array(4, 0, 0, 8, 0, 3, 0, 0, 1), _
            Array(7, 0, 0, 0, 2, 0, 0, 0, 6), _
            Array(0, 6, 0, 0, 0, 0, 2, 8, 0), _
            Array(0, 0, 0, 4, 1, 9, 0, 0, 5), _
            Array(0, 0, 0, 0, 8, 0, 0, 7, 9))


If SolveSudoku() Then
    MsgBox "Sudoku solved successfully!"
    PrintSudoku()
Else
    MsgBox "No solution found!"
End If
```

Simple Paint Program (simple_paint_program.vbs)

```vbscript
' VBScript Simple Paint Program

Dim x1, y1, x2, y2, color

Set objShell = CreateObject("WScript.Shell")

objShell.Run "mspaint.exe"

WScript.Sleep 1000 ' Wait for Paint to open

' Simulate mouse click and draw a line in Paint

x1 = 100

y1 = 100

x2 = 200

y2 = 200

color = "ff0000" ' Red color in hexadecimal format

objShell.AppActivate "Paint"

objShell.SendKeys "%FP" ' Access Paint's tools menu (Alt+F+P)

objShell.SendKeys "{RIGHT}" ' Select the pencil tool

objShell.SendKeys "~" ' Start drawing

objShell.SendKeys "{DOWN}" & x1 & "{RIGHT}" & y1 & "{DOWN}" & x2 &

"{RIGHT}" & y2 & "~" ' Draw line

objShell.SendKeys "%{F4}" ' Close Paint (Alt+F4)
```

Budget Tracker (budget_tracker.vbs)

```vbscript
' VBScript Budget Tracker

Dim totalIncome, totalExpenses, netSavings

totalIncome = CDbl(InputBox("Enter total income:"))

totalExpenses = CDbl(InputBox("Enter total expenses:"))

netSavings = totalIncome - totalExpenses
```

```vbscript
If netSavings > 0 Then
    MsgBox "You have a surplus of $" & netSavings
ElseIf netSavings < 0 Then
    MsgBox "You have a deficit of $" & Abs(netSavings)
Else
    MsgBox "Your income equals your expenses. No savings or deficit."
End If
```

Web Scraper (web_scraper.vbs)

```vbscript
' VBScript Web Scraper
Dim url, http, html

url = InputBox("Enter URL to scrape:")

Set http = CreateObject("MSXML2.ServerXMLHTTP")
http.Open "GET", url, False
http.setRequestHeader "Content-Type", "text/html"
http.send ""

If http.Status = 200 Then
    html = http.responseText
    ' Parse and extract desired content from 'html' string
    MsgBox "Web scraping successful!"
Else
    MsgBox "Error: " & http.Status & " - " & http.statusText
End If
```

Currency Exchange Rates (currency_exchange_rates.vbs)

```vbscript
' VBScript Currency Exchange Rates
Dim fromCurrency, toCurrency, amount, rate, convertedAmount
```

```vbscript
fromCurrency = InputBox("Enter source currency code:")
toCurrency = InputBox("Enter target currency code:")
amount = CDbl(InputBox("Enter amount to convert:"))

' Example exchange rate lookup (replace with actual API call)
rate = 1.2 ' Exchange rate from fromCurrency to toCurrency

convertedAmount = amount * rate
MsgBox amount & " " & fromCurrency & " = " & convertedAmount & " " &
toCurrency
```

Simple Chatbot (simple_chatbot.vbs)

```vbscript
' VBScript Simple Chatbot
Dim userInput, botResponse

userInput = InputBox("Hello! How can I assist you today?")

If InStr(userInput, "hello") > 0 Or InStr(userInput, "hi") > 0 Then
    botResponse = "Hello there! How can I help you?"
ElseIf InStr(userInput, "help") > 0 Then
    botResponse = "Sure! What do you need assistance with?"
Else
    botResponse = "I'm sorry, I didn't understand that. Can you please rephrase?"
End If

MsgBox botResponse
```

URL Encoder/Decoder (url_encoder_decoder.vbs)

```vbscript
' VBScript URL Encoder/Decoder
Dim inputURL, encodedURL, decodedURL
```

```
inputURL = InputBox("Enter URL:")

' Encode URL

encodedURL = Replace(Replace(Replace(Replace(inputURL, " ", "%20"), ":", "%3A"), "/", "%2F"), "?", "%3F")


' Decode URL

decodedURL = Replace(Replace(Replace(Replace(encodedURL, "%20", " "), "%3A", ":"), "%2F", "/"), "%3F", "?")


MsgBox "Encoded URL: " & encodedURL & vbCrLf & "Decoded URL: " & decodedURL
```

IP Address Tracker (ip_address_tracker.vbs)

```
' VBScript IP Address Tracker
Dim hostname, ipAddresses, ipAddress


hostname = InputBox("Enter hostname:")


Set objWMIService = GetObject("winmgmts:\\.\root\cimv2")
Set colItems = objWMIService.ExecQuery("Select * from
Win32_NetworkAdapterConfiguration where IPEnabled=True")


ipAddresses = ""
For Each objItem in colItems
    For Each ipAddress in objItem.IPAddress
        ipAddresses = ipAddresses & ipAddress & vbCrLf
    Next
Next


MsgBox "IP Addresses for " & hostname & ":" & vbCrLf & ipAddresses
```

Reverse a String (reverse_string.vbs)

```vbscript
' VBScript Reverse a String
Dim inputString, reversedString, i

inputString = InputBox("Enter a string:")

reversedString = ""
For i = Len(inputString) To 1 Step -1
    reversedString = reversedString & Mid(inputString, i, 1)
Next

MsgBox "Reversed String: " & reversedString
```

Number Palindrome Checker (number_palindrome_checker.vbs)

```vbscript
' VBScript Number Palindrome Checker
Dim number, originalNumber, reversedNumber

number = InputBox("Enter a number:")
originalNumber = CInt(number)

reversedNumber = 0
Do While number > 0
    reversedNumber = (reversedNumber * 10) + (number Mod 10)
    number = number \ 10
Loop

If originalNumber = reversedNumber Then
    MsgBox originalNumber & " is a palindrome!"
Else
    MsgBox originalNumber & " is not a palindrome!"
End If
```

Count Vowels and Consonants (count_vowels_consonants.vbs)

```vbscript
' VBScript Count Vowels and Consonants
Dim text, char, vowels, consonants

text = InputBox("Enter text:")
text = LCase(text) ' Convert text to lowercase for case-insensitive comparison

vowels = 0
consonants = 0

For i = 1 To Len(text)
   char = Mid(text, i, 1)
   If char Like "[aeiou]" Then
      vowels = vowels + 1
   ElseIf char >= "a" And char <= "z" Then
      consonants = consonants + 1
   End If
Next
MsgBox "Vowels: " & vowels & vbCrLf & "Consonants: " & consonants
```

Count Words in a String (count_words_in_string.vbs)

```vbscript
' VBScript Count Words in a String
Dim inputString, words

inputString = InputBox("Enter a string:")
words = Split(inputString, " ")

MsgBox "Number of words in the string: " & UBound(words) + 1
```

Merge Two Strings (merge_two_strings.vbs)

```vbscript
' VBScript Merge Two Strings
Dim string1, string2, mergedString

string1 = InputBox("Enter first string:")
string2 = InputBox("Enter second string:")

mergedString = string1 & string2
MsgBox "Merged String: " & mergedString
```

Split a String (split_string.vbs)

```vbscript
' VBScript Split a String
Dim inputString, delimiter, parts
inputString = InputBox("Enter a string:")
delimiter = InputBox("Enter delimiter to split the string:")
parts = Split(inputString, delimiter)
MsgBox "Parts of the string after splitting:" & vbCrLf & Join(parts, vbCrLf)
```

Check Anagram Strings (check_anagram_strings.vbs)

```vbscript
' VBScript Check Anagram Strings
Dim string1, string2, sortedString1, sortedString2
string1 = InputBox("Enter first string:")
string2 = InputBox("Enter second string:")
sortedString1 = SortString(string1)
sortedString2 = SortString(string2)

If sortedString1 = sortedString2 Then
    MsgBox string1 & " and " & string2 & " are anagrams!"
Else
    MsgBox string1 & " and " & string2 & " are not anagrams."
End If
```

```vbscript
Function SortString(str)
    Dim arr
    arr = Split(str, "")
    BubbleSort arr
    SortString = Join(arr, "")
End Function


Sub BubbleSort(arr)
    Dim i, j, temp
    For i = 0 To UBound(arr) - 1
        For j = 0 To UBound(arr) - i - 1
            If arr(j) > arr(j + 1) Then
                temp = arr(j)
                arr(j) = arr(j + 1)
                arr(j + 1) = temp
            End If
        Next
    Next
End Sub
```


Reverse Words in a Sentence (reverse_words_in_sentence.vbs)

```vbscript
' VBScript Reverse Words in a Sentence
Dim inputSentence, words, reversedSentence
inputSentence = InputBox("Enter a sentence:")
words = Split(inputSentence, " ")
ReDim reversedWords(UBound(words))
For i = 0 To UBound(words)
    reversedWords(i) = ReverseString(words(i))
Next
```

```vbscript
reversedSentence = Join(reversedWords, " ")
MsgBox "Reversed Words in Sentence: " & reversedSentence
Function ReverseString(str)
    Dim i, reversedStr
    For i = Len(str) To 1 Step -1
        reversedStr = reversedStr & Mid(str, i, 1)
    Next
    ReverseString = reversedStr
End Function
```

Check Pangram Sentence (check_pangram_sentence.vbs)

```vbscript
' VBScript Check Pangram Sentence
Dim inputSentence, alphabet, missingLetters, i

inputSentence = InputBox("Enter a sentence:")
alphabet = "abcdefghijklmnopqrstuvwxyz"

inputSentence = LCase(inputSentence) ' Convert sentence to lowercase for case-
insensitive comparison

missingLetters = ""
For i = 1 To Len(alphabet)
    If InStr(inputSentence, Mid(alphabet, i, 1)) = 0 Then
        missingLetters = missingLetters & Mid(alphabet, i, 1)
    End If
Next

If missingLetters = "" Then
    MsgBox "The sentence is a pangram!"
Else
    MsgBox "The sentence is not a pangram. Missing letters: " & missingLetters
```

```
End If
```

Simple RSS Reader (simple_rss_reader.vbs)

```
' VBScript Simple RSS Reader
Dim rssUrl, http, xmlDoc, itemNodes, itemTitle, itemLink, itemsList
rssUrl = InputBox("Enter RSS feed URL:")


Set http = CreateObject("MSXML2.ServerXMLHTTP")
http.Open "GET", rssUrl, False
http.setRequestHeader "Content-Type", "text/xml"
http.send ""


If http.Status = 200 Then
    Set xmlDoc = CreateObject("Microsoft.XMLDOM")
    xmlDoc.async = False
    xmlDoc.loadXML http.responseText


    Set itemNodes = xmlDoc.SelectNodes("//item")
    itemsList = "Latest articles:" & vbCrLf
    For Each itemNode In itemNodes
        itemTitle = itemNode.SelectSingleNode("title").Text
        itemLink = itemNode.SelectSingleNode("link").Text
        itemsList = itemsList & "- " & itemTitle & " (" & itemLink & ")" & vbCrLf
    Next


    MsgBox itemsList
Else
    MsgBox "Error: " & http.Status & " - " & http.statusText
End If
```

Simple Video Player (simple_video_player.vbs)

```vbscript
' VBScript Simple Video Player
Dim videoFilePath

videoFilePath = InputBox("Enter path to video file:")

If videoFilePath <> "" Then
    Set objShell = CreateObject("WScript.Shell")
    objShell.Run Chr(34) & videoFilePath & Chr(34), 1, False ' Open video file in default
media player
Else
    MsgBox "Invalid video file path."
End If
```

Text to Speech Converter (text_to_speech_converter.vbs)

```vbscript
' VBScript Text to Speech Converter
Dim textToSpeak
textToSpeak = InputBox("Enter text to convert to speech:")
If textToSpeak <> "" Then
    Set sapi = CreateObject("SAPI.SpVoice")
    sapi.Speak textToSpeak
Else
    MsgBox "No text entered."
End If
```

Voice Recorder (voice_recorder.vbs)

```vbscript
' VBScript Voice Recorder
MsgBox "Voice recording will start now. Press OK to begin."
Set soundRec = CreateObject("WMRecorderLib.WMRecorder.1")
soundRec.Profile.Mode = 0 ' Set mode to voice recording
soundRec.Profile.FileName = "recorded_voice.wav"
```

```
soundRec.Profile.Start

MsgBox "Recording in progress. Press OK to stop recording."
soundRec.Profile.Stop

MsgBox "Voice recording saved as 'recorded_voice.wav'."
```

Audio Player (audio_player.vbs)

```
' VBScript Audio Player
Dim audioFilePath
audioFilePath = InputBox("Enter path to audio file:")

If audioFilePath <> "" Then
    Set objShell = CreateObject("WScript.Shell")
    objShell.Run Chr(34) & audioFilePath & Chr(34), 1, False ' Open audio file in default
media player
Else
    MsgBox "Invalid audio file path."
End If
```

Image Viewer (image_viewer.vbs)

```
' VBScript Image Viewer
Dim imagePath
imagePath = InputBox("Enter path to image file:")

If imagePath <> "" Then
    Set objShell = CreateObject("WScript.Shell")
    objShell.Run Chr(34) & imagePath & Chr(34), 1, False ' Open image file in default
image viewer
Else
    MsgBox "Invalid image file path."
```

```
End If
```

Quiz Game (quiz_game.vbs)

```
' VBScript Quiz Game
Dim question1, question2, question3, answer1, answer2, answer3, userAnswer, score
question1 = "What is the capital of France?"
answer1 = "Paris"
question2 = "Which planet is known as the Red Planet?"
answer2 = "Mars"
question3 = "Who painted the Mona Lisa?"
answer3 = "Leonardo da Vinci"

score = 0

userAnswer = InputBox(question1)
If LCase(userAnswer) = LCase(answer1) Then score = score + 1

userAnswer = InputBox(question2)
If LCase(userAnswer) = LCase(answer2) Then score = score + 1

userAnswer = InputBox(question3)
If LCase(userAnswer) = LCase(answer3) Then score = score + 1

MsgBox "Quiz completed! Your score: " & score & " out of 3"
```

Calendar Event Reminder (calendar_event_reminder.vbs)

```
' VBScript Calendar Event Reminder
Dim eventDate, eventName, currentDate

eventDate = InputBox("Enter event date (MM/DD/YYYY):")
eventName = InputBox("Enter event name:")
```

```
currentDate = Date()

If eventDate = currentDate Then
    MsgBox "Reminder: Today is " & eventName
Else
    MsgBox "No event today. Next event: " & eventName & " on " & eventDate
End If
```

Simple IDE (simple_ide.vbs)

```
' VBScript Simple IDE
Dim filePath, fileContent

filePath = InputBox("Enter file path:")

If filePath <> "" Then
    Set objShell = CreateObject("WScript.Shell")
    objShell.Run "notepad.exe " & Chr(34) & filePath & Chr(34), 1, True ' Open file in
Notepad
Else
    MsgBox "Invalid file path."
End If
D
```

Digital Clock with Alarms (digital_clock_with_alarms.vbs)

```
' VBScript Digital Clock with Alarms
Dim alarmTime, currentTime

alarmTime = InputBox("Enter alarm time (HH:MM AM/PM):")
MsgBox "Alarm set for " & alarmTime

Do
```

```vbscript
    currentTime = Format(Now, "hh:mm AM/PM")
    If currentTime = alarmTime Then
        MsgBox "Alarm! It's " & currentTime
        Exit Do
    End If
    WScript.Sleep 1000 ' Wait for 1 second before checking again
Loop
```

Directory Size Checker (directory_size_checker.vbs)

```vbscript
' VBScript Directory Size Checker
Dim folderPath, fso, folder, totalSize

folderPath = InputBox("Enter directory path:")

If folderPath <> "" Then
    Set fso = CreateObject("Scripting.FileSystemObject")
    If fso.FolderExists(folderPath) Then
        Set folder = fso.GetFolder(folderPath)
        totalSize = folder.Size / 1024 ' Convert bytes to kilobytes
        MsgBox "Size of " & folderPath & ": " & FormatNumber(totalSize, 2) & " KB"
    Else
        MsgBox "Directory not found."
    End If
Else
    MsgBox "Invalid directory path."
End If
```

Check File Permissions (check_file_permissions.vbs)

```vbscript
' VBScript Check File Permissions
Dim filePath, fso, file, attributes
```

```vbscript
filePath = InputBox("Enter file path:")

If filePath <> "" Then
    Set fso = CreateObject("Scripting.FileSystemObject")
    If fso.FileExists(filePath) Then
        Set file = fso.GetFile(filePath)
        attributes = ""
        If file.Attributes And 1 Then attributes = attributes & "Read-Only, "
        If file.Attributes And 2 Then attributes = attributes & "Hidden, "
        If file.Attributes And 4 Then attributes = attributes & "System, "
        If file.Attributes And 32 Then attributes = attributes & "Archive, "

        If attributes <> "" Then
            attributes = Left(attributes, Len(attributes) - 2) ' Remove trailing comma and space
            MsgBox "File permissions for " & filePath & ": " & attributes
        Else
            MsgBox "No special permissions set for " & filePath
        End If
    Else
        MsgBox "File not found."
    End If
Else
    MsgBox "Invalid file path."
End If
```

System Information Tool (system_information_tool.vbs)

```vbscript
' VBScript System Information Tool
Dim systemInfo

Set objWMIService = GetObject("winmgmts:\\.\root\cimv2")
```

```vbscript
Set systemInfo = objWMIService.ExecQuery("SELECT * FROM
Win32_ComputerSystem")

For Each info In systemInfo
    MsgBox "System Information:" & vbCrLf & _
        "Manufacturer: " & info.Manufacturer & vbCrLf & _
        "Model: " & info.Model & vbCrLf & _
        "Total Physical Memory: " & FormatNumber(info.TotalPhysicalMemory / 1024 /
1024, 0) & " MB" & vbCrLf & _
        "Number of Processors: " & info.NumberOfProcessors
Next
```

Prime Factorization (prime_factorization.vbs)

```vbscript
' VBScript Prime Factorization
Dim number, i

number = InputBox("Enter a number to find its prime factors:")
i = 2

While number > 1
    If number Mod i = 0 Then
        MsgBox i
        number = number / i
    Else
        i = i + 1
    End If
Wend
```

GCD (Greatest Common Divisor) Calculator (gcd_calculator.vbs)

```vbscript
' VBScript GCD (Greatest Common Divisor) Calculator
Dim num1, num2, temp
```

```vbscript
num1 = InputBox("Enter first number:")
num2 = InputBox("Enter second number:")

Do While num2 <> 0
    temp = num1 Mod num2
    num1 = num2
    num2 = temp
Loop

MsgBox "GCD of " & num1 & " and " & num2 & " is: " & num1
```

LCM (Least Common Multiple) Calculator (lcm_calculator.vbs)

```vbscript
' VBScript LCM (Least Common Multiple) Calculator
Dim num1, num2, gcd, lcm

num1 = InputBox("Enter first number:")
num2 = InputBox("Enter second number:")

' Calculate GCD
Do While num2 <> 0
    temp = num1 Mod num2
    num1 = num2
    num2 = temp
Loop
gcd = num1

' Calculate LCM using GCD
lcm = (Input1 * Input2) / gcd

MsgBox "LCM of " & Input1 & " and " & Input2 & " is: " & lcm
```

Permutations and Combinations Calculator (permutations_combinations_calculator.vbs)

```vbscript
' VBScript Permutations and Combinations Calculator
Dim n, r, permutations, combinations

n = InputBox("Enter total items (n):")
r = InputBox("Enter items to choose (r):")

' Calculate permutations (nPr)
permutations = Factorial(n) / Factorial(n - r)

' Calculate combinations (nCr)
combinations = Factorial(n) / (Factorial(r) * Factorial(n - r))

MsgBox "Permutations (nPr): " & permutations & vbCrLf & "Combinations (nCr): " & combinations

Function Factorial(num)
    If num <= 1 Then
        Factorial = 1
    Else
        Factorial = num * Factorial(num - 1)
    End If
End Function
```

Dice Simulation (dice_simulation.vbs)

```vbscript
' VBScript Dice Simulation
Dim numThrows, results, i

Randomize
numThrows = InputBox("Enter number of dice throws:")
```

```vbscript
results = ""
For i = 1 To numThrows
    results = results & "Throw " & i & ": " & Int((6 * Rnd) + 1) & vbCrLf
Next


MsgBox "Dice Simulation Results:" & vbCrLf & results
```

Movie Ticket Booking System (movie_ticket_booking_system.vbs)

```vbscript
' VBScript Movie Ticket Booking System
Dim movieName, numTickets, totalPrice
movieName = InputBox("Enter movie name:")
numTickets = InputBox("Enter number of tickets:")


' Assuming ticket price is $10 per ticket
totalPrice = numTickets * 10


MsgBox "Movie: " & movieName & vbCrLf & _
    "Number of Tickets: " & numTickets & vbCrLf & _
    "Total Price: $" & totalPrice
```

Employee Management System (employee_management_system.vbs)

```vbscript
' VBScript Employee Management System
Dim employees(3, 2)
Dim i


' Populate employees array with sample data
employees(0, 0) = "John"
employees(0, 1) = "Doe"
employees(0, 2) = "Manager"
```

```
employees(1, 0) = "Jane"

employees(1, 1) = "Smith"

employees(1, 2) = "Developer"


employees(2, 0) = "Alice"

employees(2, 1) = "Johnson"

employees(2, 2) = "Designer"


employees(3, 0) = "Bob"

employees(3, 1) = "Brown"

employees(3, 2) = "Support"


' Display employee details
For i = 0 To UBound(employees, 1)
    MsgBox "Employee " & (i + 1) & ": " & vbCrLf & _
        "Name: " & employees(i, 0) & " " & employees(i, 1) & vbCrLf & _
        "Role: " & employees(i, 2)
Next
```

Bank Management System (bank_management_system.vbs)

```
' VBScript Bank Management System
Dim customerName, accountNumber, balance


customerName = InputBox("Enter customer name:")

accountNumber = InputBox("Enter account number:")

balance = CDbl(InputBox("Enter current balance:"))


Do

    Dim choice, amount


    choice = InputBox("Bank Management System Menu:" & vbCrLf & _
```

```vbscript
            "1. Deposit" & vbCrLf & _
            "2. Withdraw" & vbCrLf & _
            "3. Check Balance" & vbCrLf & _
            "4. Exit" & vbCrLf & _
            "Enter your choice:")


    Select Case choice
        Case "1"
            amount = CDbl(InputBox("Enter amount to deposit:"))
            balance = balance + amount
            MsgBox "Amount deposited successfully. Current balance: " & balance
        Case "2"
            amount = CDbl(InputBox("Enter amount to withdraw:"))
            If amount > balance Then
                MsgBox "Insufficient balance. Withdrawal failed."
            Else
                balance = balance - amount
                MsgBox "Amount withdrawn successfully. Current balance: " & balance
            End If
        Case "3"
            MsgBox "Current balance: " & balance
        Case "4"
            MsgBox "Exiting Bank Management System. Thank you!"
            Exit Do
        Case Else
            MsgBox "Invalid choice. Please try again."
    End Select
Loop
```

Library Management System (library_management_system.vbs)

```vbscript
' VBScript Library Management System
Dim books(3, 2)
Dim i, bookTitle, authorName, availableCopies, choice, bookFound

' Populate books array with sample data
books(0, 0) = "Harry Potter and the Sorcerer's Stone"
books(0, 1) = "J.K. Rowling"
books(0, 2) = 5 ' 5 copies available

books(1, 0) = "To Kill a Mockingbird"
books(1, 1) = "Harper Lee"
books(1, 2) = 3 ' 3 copies available

books(2, 0) = "The Great Gatsby"
books(2, 1) = "F. Scott Fitzgerald"
books(2, 2) = 2 ' 2 copies available

books(3, 0) = "1984"
books(3, 1) = "George Orwell"
books(3, 2) = 4 ' 4 copies available

Do
    bookTitle = InputBox("Enter book title to borrow or return (or 'exit' to quit):")
    bookFound = False

    If LCase(bookTitle) = "exit" Then
        MsgBox "Exiting Library Management System. Thank you!"
        Exit Do
    End If
```

```vbscript
For i = 0 To UBound(books, 1)
    If LCase(books(i, 0)) = LCase(bookTitle) Then
        bookFound = True
        availableCopies = books(i, 2)


        choice = InputBox("Book '" & books(i, 0) & "' by " & books(i, 1) & " is available with " & availableCopies & " copies." & vbCrLf & _
                "1. Borrow a copy" & vbCrLf & _
                "2. Return a copy" & vbCrLf & _
                "Enter your choice:")


        Select Case choice
            Case "1"
                If availableCopies > 0 Then
                    books(i, 2) = availableCopies - 1
                    MsgBox "Book borrowed successfully. Remaining copies: " & books(i, 2)
                Else
                    MsgBox "No copies available for borrowing."
                End If
            Case "2"
                books(i, 2) = availableCopies + 1
                MsgBox "Book returned successfully. Remaining copies: " & books(i, 2)
            Case Else
                MsgBox "Invalid choice. Please try again."
        End Select
        Exit For
    End If
Next


If Not bookFound Then
```

```
        MsgBox "Book '" & bookTitle & "' not found in the library."
    End If
Loop
```

Online Shopping System (online_shopping_system.vbs)

```
' VBScript Online Shopping System
Dim products(3, 1)
Dim i, productName, productPrice, choice, productFound
' Populate products array with sample data
products(0, 0) = "Laptop"
products(0, 1) = 1200

products(1, 0) = "Smartphone"
products(1, 1) = 800

products(2, 0) = "Headphones"
products(2, 1) = 100

products(3, 0) = "Bluetooth Speaker"
products(3, 1) = 150

Do
    productName = InputBox("Enter product name to add to cart (or 'exit' to quit):")
    productFound = False

    If LCase(productName) = "exit" Then
        MsgBox "Exiting Online Shopping System. Thank you!"
        Exit Do
    End If

    For i = 0 To UBound(products, 1)
```

```vbscript
        If LCase(products(i, 0)) = LCase(productName) Then
            productFound = True
            productPrice = products(i, 1)

            choice = InputBox("Product '" & products(i, 0) & "' is available for $" &
productPrice & "." & vbCrLf & _
                    "1. Add to Cart" & vbCrLf & _
                    "Enter your choice:")

            If choice = "1" Then
                MsgBox "Product added to cart successfully."
            Else
                MsgBox "Invalid choice. Please try again."
            End If
            Exit For
        End If
    Next

    If Not productFound Then
        MsgBox "Product '" & productName & "' not found."
    End If
Loop
```

Hotel Management System (hotel_management_system.vbs)

```vbscript
' VBScript Hotel Management System
Dim rooms(5), roomNumber, choice

' Initialize rooms availability (0 = available, 1 = occupied)
For i = 1 To 5
    rooms(i) = 0
Next
```

```vbscript
Do
    choice = InputBox("Hotel Management System Menu:" & vbCrLf & _
            "1. Check-In" & vbCrLf & _
            "2. Check-Out" & vbCrLf & _
            "3. Display Room Status" & vbCrLf & _
            "4. Exit" & vbCrLf & _
            "Enter your choice:")


    Select Case choice
      Case "1"
        roomNumber = InputBox("Enter room number to check-in:")
        If rooms(roomNumber) = 0 Then
          rooms(roomNumber) = 1
          MsgBox "Room " & roomNumber & " checked-in successfully."
        Else
          MsgBox "Room " & roomNumber & " is already occupied."
        End If
      Case "2"
        roomNumber = InputBox("Enter room number to check-out:")
        If rooms(roomNumber) = 1 Then
          rooms(roomNumber) = 0
          MsgBox "Room " & roomNumber & " checked-out successfully."
        Else
          MsgBox "Room " & roomNumber & " is not occupied."
        End If
      Case "3"
        Dim status
        status = "Room Status:" & vbCrLf
        For i = 1 To 5
```

```vbscript
        status = status & "Room " & i & ": " & IIf(rooms(i) = 0, "Available",
"Occupied") & vbCrLf
        Next
        MsgBox status
      Case "4"
        MsgBox "Exiting Hotel Management System. Thank you!"
        Exit Do
      Case Else
        MsgBox "Invalid choice. Please try again."
    End Select
Loop
```

Create and Read JSON Files (create_read_json_files.vbs)

```vbscript
' VBScript Create and Read JSON Files
Dim jsonObject, jsonData, fileSystem, fileObject, filePath
' Create a JSON object
Set jsonObject = CreateObject("Scripting.Dictionary")
jsonObject.Add "name", "John Doe"
jsonObject.Add "age", 30
jsonObject.Add "city", "New York"

' Convert JSON object to string
jsonData = Join(Array("{", """name"": """ & jsonObject("name") & """,", _
          """age"": " & jsonObject("age") & ",", _
          """city"": """ & jsonObject("city") & """}", ""), "")

' Write JSON data to a file
filePath = "data.json"
Set fileSystem = CreateObject("Scripting.FileSystemObject")
Set fileObject = fileSystem.CreateTextFile(filePath, True)
fileObject.Write jsonData
```

```vbscript
fileObject.Close


' Read JSON data from the file
Set fileObject = fileSystem.OpenTextFile(filePath, 1)
jsonData = fileObject.ReadAll
fileObject.Close


MsgBox "JSON data read from file:" & vbCrLf & jsonData
```

Temperature Conversion Tool (temperature_conversion_tool.vbs)

```vbscript
' VBScript Temperature Conversion Tool
Dim choice, value, result


choice = InputBox("Temperature Conversion Tool:" & vbCrLf & _
        "1. Celsius to Fahrenheit" & vbCrLf & _
        "2. Fahrenheit to Celsius" & vbCrLf & _
        "Enter your choice:")


Select Case choice
   Case "1"
     value = CDbl(InputBox("Enter temperature in Celsius:"))
     result = (value * 9 / 5) + 32
     MsgBox value & " Celsius = " & result & " Fahrenheit"
   Case "2"
     value = CDbl(InputBox("Enter temperature in Fahrenheit:"))
     result = (value - 32) * 5 / 9
     MsgBox value & " Fahrenheit = " & result & " Celsius"
   Case Else
     MsgBox "Invalid choice. Please try again."
End Select
```

Distance Conversion Tool (distance_conversion_tool.vbs)

```vbscript
' VBScript Distance Conversion Tool

Dim choice, value, result

choice = InputBox("Distance Conversion Tool:" & vbCrLf & _
          "1. Miles to Kilometers" & vbCrLf & _
          "2. Kilometers to Miles" & vbCrLf & _
          "Enter your choice:")

Select Case choice
    Case "1"
        value = CDbl(InputBox("Enter distance in miles:"))
        result = value * 1.60934
        MsgBox value & " miles = " & result & " kilometers"
    Case "2"
        value = CDbl(InputBox("Enter distance in kilometers:"))
        result = value / 1.60934
        MsgBox value & " kilometers = " & result & " miles"
    Case Else
        MsgBox "Invalid choice. Please try again."
End Select
```

Calculator with GUI (calculator_with_gui.vbs)

```vbscript
' VBScript Calculator with GUI
' This script demonstrates a basic calculator using InputBox for user input and message
boxes for displaying results.

Dim firstNumber, secondNumber, operation, result

firstNumber = CDbl(InputBox("Enter first number:"))
operation = InputBox("Enter operation (+, -, *, /):")
```

```vbscript
secondNumber = CDbl(InputBox("Enter second number:"))


Select Case operation
   Case "+"
      result = firstNumber + secondNumber
   Case "-"
      result = firstNumber - secondNumber
   Case "*"
      result = firstNumber * secondNumber
   Case "/"
      If secondNumber <> 0 Then
         result = firstNumber / secondNumber
      Else
         MsgBox "Error: Division by zero!"
         WScript.Quit
      End If
   Case Else
      MsgBox "Invalid operation. Please try again."
      WScript.Quit
End Select


MsgBox "Result: " & result
```

File Explorer (file_explorer.vbs)

```vbscript
' VBScript File Explorer
Set objShell = CreateObject("Shell.Application")
objShell.Explore("C:\") ' Change to desired directory path
```

Text File Search Utility (text_file_search_utility.vbs)

```vbscript
' VBScript Text File Search Utility
Dim filePath, searchString, fileContent, fileObject

filePath = InputBox("Enter path to text file:")
searchString = InputBox("Enter search string:")

If filePath <> "" And searchString <> "" Then
    Set fileObject = CreateObject("Scripting.FileSystemObject").OpenTextFile(filePath)
    fileContent = fileObject.ReadAll
    fileObject.Close

    If InStr(1, fileContent, searchString, vbTextCompare) > 0 Then
        MsgBox "Search string found in the text file."
    Else
        MsgBox "Search string not found in the text file."
    End If
Else
    MsgBox "Invalid input. Please provide valid file path and search string."
End If
```

Unit Conversion Tool (unit_conversion_tool.vbs)

```vbscript
' VBScript Unit Conversion Tool
Dim choice, value, result
choice = InputBox("Unit Conversion Tool:" & vbCrLf & _
        "1. Pounds to Kilograms" & vbCrLf & _
        "2. Kilograms to Pounds" & vbCrLf & _
        "Enter your choice:")
Select Case choice
    Case "1"
        value = CDbl(InputBox("Enter weight in pounds:"))
```

```
    result = value * 0.453592
    MsgBox value & " pounds = " & result & " kilograms"
  Case "2"
    value = CDbl(InputBox("Enter weight in kilograms:"))
    result = value / 0.453592
    MsgBox value & " kilograms = " & result & " pounds"
  Case Else
    MsgBox "Invalid choice. Please try again."
End Select
```

Volume Conversion Tool (volume_conversion_tool.vbs)

```
' VBScript Volume Conversion Tool
Dim choice, value, result

choice = InputBox("Volume Conversion Tool:" & vbCrLf & _
        "1. Liters to Gallons" & vbCrLf & _
        "2. Gallons to Liters" & vbCrLf & _
        "Enter your choice:")

Select Case choice
  Case "1"
    value = CDbl(InputBox("Enter volume in liters:"))
    result = value * 0.264172
    MsgBox value & " liters = " & result & " gallons"
  Case "2"
    value = CDbl(InputBox("Enter volume in gallons:"))
    result = value / 0.264172
    MsgBox value & " gallons – " & result & " liters"
  Case Else
    MsgBox "Invalid choice. Please try again."
End Select
```

Photo Viewer (photo_viewer.vbs)

```vbscript
' VBScript Photo Viewer
Dim objShell, objFSO, objFolder, objFiles, objFile
Dim folderPath, file, filePath, imageExtensions, i

' Specify the folder path containing images
folderPath = "C:\Path\To\Your\Images"

' Create necessary objects
Set objShell = CreateObject("WScript.Shell")
Set objFSO = CreateObject("Scripting.FileSystemObject")

' Check if the folder path exists
If objFSO.FolderExists(folderPath) Then
    ' Get the folder object
    Set objFolder = objFSO.GetFolder(folderPath)
    Set objFiles = objFolder.Files

    ' Define supported image extensions
    imageExtensions = Array(".jpg", ".jpeg", ".png", ".gif", ".bmp")

    ' Loop through each file in the folder
    For Each objFile in objFiles
        ' Check if the file is an image based on the extension
        For i = LBound(imageExtensions) To UBound(imageExtensions)
            If LCase(objFSO.GetExtensionName(objFile.Name)) =
LCase(Mid(imageExtensions(i), 2)) Then
                filePath = objFile.Path
                ' Use default image viewer to display the image
                objShell.Run """" & filePath & """", 1, False
                Exit For
```

```vbscript
        End If
      Next
    Next
  Else
    MsgBox "Folder not found: " & folderPath
  End If
```

Email Sender (email_sender.vbs)

```vbscript
' VBScript Email Sender
Dim objOutlook, objMail

' Create Outlook application object
Set objOutlook = CreateObject("Outlook.Application")

' Create a new mail item
Set objMail = objOutlook.CreateItem(0)

' Set email properties
objMail.To = "recipient@example.com"
objMail.Subject = "Test Email from VBScript"
objMail.Body = "This is a test email sent using VBScript."

' Send the email
objMail.Send

' Display confirmation message
MsgBox "Email sent successfully."
```

Barcode Generator (barcode_generator.vbs)

```vbscript
' VBScript Barcode Generator
Dim objShell, barcodeText, tempFilePath

' Set barcode text
barcodeText = InputBox("Enter text for barcode:")

' Generate a temporary text file with barcode text
Set objFSO = CreateObject("Scripting.FileSystemObject")
tempFilePath = objFSO.GetSpecialFolder(2) & "\barcode.txt"
Set objFile = objFSO.CreateTextFile(tempFilePath, True)
objFile.Write barcodeText
objFile.Close

' Use a command-line tool to generate barcode image from the text file
Set objShell = CreateObject("WScript.Shell")
objShell.Run "cmd /c barcode-generator.exe -i " & tempFilePath & " -o barcode.png", 0, True

' Display the generated barcode image
objShell.Run "barcode.png", 1, False

' Delete the temporary text file
objFSO.DeleteFile(tempFilePath)
```

Report Generator (report_generator.vbs)

```vbscript
' VBScript Report Generator
Dim objFSO, objFile, reportData, reportFilePath

' Sample report data (can be obtained from database or file)
reportData = "Sample Report Data:" & vbCrLf & _
```

```vbscript
    "1. Item 1: $10" & vbCrLf & _
    "2. Item 2: $20" & vbCrLf & _
    "3. Item 3: $30" & vbCrLf & _
    "Total: $60"


' Specify the report file path
reportFilePath = "C:\Path\To\Your\Report.txt"


' Create a text file and write report data to it
Set objFSO = CreateObject("Scripting.FileSystemObject")
Set objFile = objFSO.CreateTextFile(reportFilePath, True)
objFile.Write reportData
objFile.Close


' Display confirmation message
MsgBox "Report generated successfully at: " & reportFilePath
```